CROW

For Ted

and in memory of the fathers:

Peter Grootendorst (1924-1997)
Jack Goodden (1914-2003)
Tito Hoogland (1925-2010)

Crow

Cornelia Hoogland

Black Moss Press
2011

Library and Archives Canada Cataloguing in Publication

Hoogland, Cornelia
Crow / Cornelia Hoogland.

Poems.
ISBN 978-0-88753-487-4

I. Title.

PS8565.O6515C76 2011   C811'.54   C2011-901309-6

Cover art: Colleen Couves, detail from *Crow Vision 1*.

Design: Kate Hargreaves

Published by Black Moss Press at 2450 Byng Road, Windsor,
Ontario, N8W 3E8 Canada. Black Moss books are distributed
in Canada and the U.S. by LitDistCo. All orders should be
directed there.

Black Moss Press books can also be found on our website
www.blackmosspress.com.

Black Moss would like to acknowledge the generous financial
support from both the Canada Council of the Arts and the
Ontario Arts Council.

PRINTED IN CANADA

contents

Writing With A Stick

Her Familiar

1.

Is crow. Watch him
peril the backyard,
hustle the birds: who
gets what/when at the feeder.
In crow's shadow
squirrel stops on a dime,
splays his body
against the tree, becomes

bark. But when
it comes to the dog, crow
fluffs his throat feathers,
tin-soldiers along the fence rail,
caws for the beagle's attention. Ups
the volume (P. Diddy

on the boom box) before stashing
a rancid morsel — you still with me dog? —
between logs in the woodpile.
Flies to his branch in the walnut
to watch what happens

next. Crow is interested.

Crow shows another point
of view, a more-than-human angle
from which to learn air
and invisible, electric currents.
From this high, factories
fracture into colour
                    and it's clear

everything's animate,
everything moves.
The light of the world through oil and water.

And his humour — his bald caw caw
obscene as your mother's moans
from the guest bedroom
the night her boyfriend sleeps over.

-2.

The thing that wakes
her: a phrase, a rhythm,
a word
      dropped
like a coat
to the floor.

In the nest of her bed,
eyes closed, skin
of pillow meeting her own,
sheet's lingering
warmth. It starts before
that, before
the garbage truck beeps
its backward quarrel down the lane,
before the light of the snow plow arcs
blue over the wall.

She jerks to sitting,
a straight-up antenna alert
and reaching, mole-blind
for that thing with a stab

of presence, with this moment in it.

She gets up to look for it as she might the dog.

Has he spent the night
in his basket under the bookshelves? Or
coiled like a fiddlehead
on the kitchen mat?

Sometimes on the landing,
on his way up the stairs, she bumps
into him. Or is he
meeting her, halfway?

3.

Because she has as many names for her children
as there are names for snow.

Because snow is both flannel-warm and stark white.
Because sparkling, glistening cold makes walking treacherous.
Because of ice puddles and flakes' holy symmetry.
Because a wildcat frost can level the garden.

She tries to write about her son, her daughters.

In the black walnut crow
screeches as he swoops through icy branches.

4.

Her lovers have taken new wives
or gone back to the old.
Pain no longer requires anything of her.

And the children — they
bind up the sorrow
they carry into the world.
In their hands it is a strength.

                              Crow

pounds at the window, flies to the power

line. Hangs from his bill,
                              hangs

upside down,
flips over, flies off.

She's ready to work.

Story of Art, 1

Begins with a three-year-old girl,
an itchy palm,
and where are my flip-flops
yelled at top volume.

The garden as she left it, squash
tossing its rumpled Kleenex flowers.

Her eyes see what her hand wants.
Bricks. Fifteen or so
line the herb garden
beside the shed.
Her fingers barely
span the width of the brick
she lifts — lid off a pan
and
         hundreds of thousands of
crickets and pill bugs
scuttle for cover.

What she makes happen. The world

yelling back.

Story of Art, 2

I'm running over the Dundas Street bridge
that crosses the Thames river,
gravel-grey and making no demands,

when a heron —
a check mark of attention,
a pencil stroke
marking a great line in a book — shoots up.

It's the first day of fall —
not the calendar's first, but the weather's.
The sky's a floured breadboard,
the clouds punchy as dough,
when a sudden, heroic
hurry of leaves, traffic
pummeling the cliffs
into town, squirrels
zippering shut the trees.

In grade five I lost
a whole season trolling
bonfire leaves, the reddest, the orangest,
got lost in the honey smell
of ironing nature between sheets of waxed paper,
lost in scotch-taping onto the window

new arrangements. The raw
sound I heard came from
me, it was crow
searching for
lit things, for the shine
of things.

Especially O, Especially Darling

Cloth swelling and
thinning, long-fibrous cloud
fast-forwarding, now
blocking the sun
that runs the length
of the beach, slips
away — as the mother too

will go — leaving a girl and an ache
big as land.

O darling girl, three good
words nestled in the last
wind-loosened days,
the one
thing a mother can promise

her daughter tossing up
the bed's milky covers,
Raffi's singable songs
by heart, smell of pancakes
on the griddle, head
out-of-bed-over-heels:
when does childhood end?

You'll love sex, says the mother.

What has the daughter done with that?
Ask her. But the mother
clings to that high tide
below Burnaby mountain

though the words are lost.

A Daughter's Heartbreak and the Fake Orgasms of Carp

The female carp can fake up to nine orgasms
as a way of staving off unwanted males.
They wiggle their tails and the males, excited
as boys with wide nets in big water, spill
their seed. Are there eggs to fertilize?
The boys are already off to the pub to brag.

Back in the bay the female spots a male thrashing toward her.
She gives him the once-over
and fakes it again — or not. She's practicing selection.

The other story is harder to write.
You hate to see your daughter hurt.
Suddenly the stakes seem high.
You can tell she's thinking marriage —
not necessarily him and not right away —
but dating's more than a good time.
She may even want the starter home
with its picket fence — you had it, once.

Still far off babies
azure-eyed as your daughter
wave their pale arms toward her, skiff
the wide blue.

All spring, weekends are punctuated
by through-the-night phone calls and crying.
The regular but ragged lines of waves.
She knows only this: she can't
share him. She's practicing
selection.

Do I hear begging?

Just the pulse
of engines, the push
of the sea.

Borrowed, in Cuba

Their padded legs
like folding chairs buckle
as they slide,
angle a save
on a hot January day
in the playing fields above Matanzas.

#5 is smallest of these girls.
Her braids lie flat
against her pretty head,
wool socks protect
her shins.

Danielle carried number #5
Grade 1 through university.

One day you're the mom
driving to soccer, to swimming,
and the next you're staring
at a quick ball
off the instep of a girl tense
with future — passing
so close you can reach out, brush

a wild ginseng of memory:
taproot groping its gingery hair
into a country not your own,
borrowed weather.

Wo ist die wolle?
(Beck's store, Munich)

I'm so far from home
that I need to stick my nose in a ball of wool.
Smell lanolin.

I ask the fraulein, Wo ist die wolle?
Sad, penetrating words scored
for a requiem. She stares
like I'm from Mars.

Because I'm serious I tuck in my arms
at my sides, pantomime
knitting, wool over needle —

her caged eyes lift. Ahhh-so, she says.
I listen for links, rechts, and the level —
probably zweite or dritte, walk in the direction
her finger points. O Wo
ist die wolle? — then see
the coloured skeins in plastic bins and I fall

into a field on a windy March day —
rubber boots and a handmade coat,
wind's needling cold through purl and knit.

Makes the girl run over the cow field.
Makes me buy wool, cast on tight stitches.

Tsunami

How good to see blue from our bed
I said from behind you, where — like a comma,
a bracket closing, the husband-half of the sentence —
I curved close as possible.
You were all I asked for. You were
Nearer My God (the ship's orchestra playing,
the Titanic sinking) To Thee.

I gave you words: marmalade, chip wagon,
football, also the French makiage,
and you gave me thwack,
vicissitude, peahen,
and from your inner acoustic,
hurricane. The afternoon

was a drug we fell into. My hair
grew an inch, your thighs grew leaner.

When our bodies parted they knew
the marrow of being together.

You walked slowly back to your studio and took up
your paintbrush (your rigger, your reservoir)
and I got to the store minutes before it closed
and bought dog food, cheese and coffee
for our life together. This life we snatch

from within an inch of drowning.

My Mother Meets Ted

He's not the first I've brought home
since the divorce.
My mother doesn't ask a single question.

Late afternoon, we're walking the spit
through a heads-up valley of fennel
the Chinese who worked the fish plant
seeded here at the turn of the century.
We breathe the yellow burst
of biscotti-butter herb.

My mother grabs a handful, rubs
the fragrant plant between her palms,
then drops it. She offers Ted
empty hands.
                    He bends
toward her, catches
her hands in his, inhales.

His body supplicant.

Our Bodies are in the Fields of Us
(after Hildegard of Bingen who said that our bodies are in our souls)

Sometimes the fields had snow on them
and were the quiet of suede
boots in a row beside the door.
But mostly the fields were dotted
with Holsteins grazing spring
grass, loud-green as girls.

Our pasture was bordered
by a ditch so wide
a person could row a small boat
between the rushes that lined the shores,
though only ducks paddled the soupy algae.
Any minute a child might
slip the banks
and drown.

       I ran.

       The fields were calling.

I wanted their cow pies, saltlicks,
their size. Where they began,
where they ended.

The Sumas Prairie, my first
eternity. At the barbed-wire gate —

field upon field.

That's how it was when I entered
the field of you.
          Ground
to land on.

Sometimes seed falls on rock
or into blackberry bushes
and gets crowded out,
but with you — lucky seed.

I am a child in yellow boots, running.

Cornelia Hoogland

Tar Baby

In the winter of 2003 Canadians grew tense at the threats of war, and wondered if their country would follow America into Iraq. For two weeks that January Crow came to visit the mirror tacked on the fence behind a backyard sculpture. His daily assaults on the mirror (that although extreme, fit into the category of mating behaviour) echoed the 6 o'clock news with its reports of fundamental postures and rumours of war.

One for sorrow

Two for joy

Three for marriage

Four for a boy

Five for silver

Six for gold

Seven a secret

Not to be told.

In Newfoundland
we're birds of omen, says Crow.

We count. People count on us.

Day 1

Crow
hops from the garden sculpture
onto the snow-crusted
flower bed
to better
dash his body
against his mirrored
rival.

Thwack.

Seven times he ricochets
off this O-so-canny
doppelganger:
scales his double's outermost
parts.

His bird feathers
gleam, are beads
of sweat
on a boxer's face.

Wings wide, Crow
hangs on,
drops against the ropes,
paces,
pumps his chest,
caws in four directions.

Day 2

Throat hackles, head feathers
puff into a ceremonial headdress.
Lower body swells, a ruffled skirt.

A territorial thing —
despite the calendar it's mild
as mating season.
Corvus Triumphanus
is up for it.

But not the sparrows
in the wisteria
above this one-man show.
Not the juncos nor the cardinal
red as Christmas
on the bleached fence post,
not Ted in his studio
cutting glass, not me
at my computer.

Day 3

Crow jabs at bits of snow and ice,
packs his beak like he's stuffing
an explosive
aimed for the mirror.

Plan B: Penetrate the mirror from atop the sculpture.

Day 4

Crow unfurls his black belt,
whips it, frays it —
wears it thin as ribbon.

Kick boxes
the glass from which
the enemy
springs his ambush.

Crow's feathers, charred
sticks.

In Bed, Night 4

We should do something.

Sleep is something.

You should stop this Crow.

Stop him?

He's going to break his neck.

I write about Crow.

It's the mirror. If it weren't there —

Take it down.

Unnn.

What do you mean unnn? Is that no? Speak up.

The sculpture doesn't work without it. The whole thing's about reflection.

So. You want me to stop Crow from gazing into the mirror so that your artwork isn't disturbed — is that right?

Well, what about you?

Me?

You're making art from somebody else's misery.

Listen, I need to get some sleep.

Crow attacks himself, and you find that 'interesting.'

It's not like I'm corrupting him.

You benefit. Don't you feel guilty, taking notes?

Not until now.

You don't want blood on your hands.

Like Crow would fulfill mother nature's plan for him if it weren't for poetry? Cute, that's really cute.

In the black walnut tree, Night 4

Before you judge me: imagine your perfect rival.

You're in combat,
about to unveil the Top Secret
you've been keeping
under wraps
for just this moment.
And there he is, your rival,
with the same small range ordinance,

also in military black serge —
an Other
as big, as carrion
as you.
Tail feathers perfectly matched.

You'd be rattled.

In battle you learn to answer
quickly, to lift off quickly,
to take and return fire,
assemble in secret, move in,
but here, with him,
it's rigged.

A smooth cold surface intervenes.
A silver sheet
drops.

A mirror? This is madness.

Day 5

The enemy persists.

Caw caw caw.

Crow's body heaves
with each vocalization
and now he swivels upside down,
claws akimbo.

He reaches across the tempered glass,
wipes clear a spot,

an opening.
It clouds — he wipes again.

Crow doesn't get the mirror.
Why should he?
Anything human is to his detriment.

Day 6

In sky above
black walnuts
urban geese hold a roughly V-shaped
mid-air flock-think.

Loud nasal honks.

They decide against
south, settle
for Wonder Bread
crumbs at the fork
of the Thames.

Migratory instincts
reduced to restlessness,
an impulse to fly —

where?

In the black walnut tree, Day 7

Humans built the highway east to west
as the crow flies.

That's why we crows —
St. John's to Victoria —
Adopt a Highway.
We feel responsible.
Each to our own
stretch of tar and engine oil.

Why we're beholden
to bits of glass
and glinty tin, metallic
puddles that taste iron,
reflect a cloudless sky.

We like the way our wings
close over our backs.
Tidy uniforms.
Our patrol's the littoral:
that zone between
the highway's mindless metal buzz and
Lake Superior.

And in our border town
we like the way heat
in flinty
layers cooks
the carrion rabbit,
the porcupine.

The way
our feet leave prints
in sand

like arrows pointing.

Day 8

Snowed during the night.
Bird's black tuxedo punctuates
the passing white phenomenon.
An old movie. Film Noir.

Crow tries to stare his enemy down.
The fiercer he — the fiercer it.
Then the dumb head-bashing.
The deep, rasping calls.

Ted Hughes writes:
"His wings are the stiff back
of his only book,
Himself the only
page —
of solid ink."

Surely such perfect
mirroring of oneself
becomes tedious?

In bed, Night 8

You sleeping?

I'm remembering somebody's Siamese fighting fish.

        Charlie.

Yeah, Charlie. Past tense.

        He died.

That's it? You don't remember rigging up a mirror outside his aquarium, watching him smash his head against the glass?

        He couldn't help himself.

You killed yourself laughing —

        What Charlie saw as a threat —

Just your masculine nature, cranked up a notch.

        He'd puff his cheeks, his chest —

A real "B" western —

        It perked him up. He needed it.

playing itself out.

        But he never learned.

Hey, that's good. I can use that.

Cornelia Hoogland

Day 9

Time to give everybody a rest.

Ted tacks a towel into the wooden frame
of a summer screen,
props it against the mirror.

Crow investigates.
A triumphant caw and up he spirals.
On a high branch he cocks
his head first to one side, then the other.
This stout general's not letting go.

He banks, he
folds his wings, he
shoots, he —
claims the sculpture-throne,
snaps off the towel,
deposes the god.

A darker, more distant
rival glints
back through wire mesh.
Through a screen darkly.

From behind my computer
(I'd gotten back to work),
I realize this crow is hard-wired.
Is going to need a withdrawal program.

Day 10

I want to release this tar baby.

I want to see what happens next.
I want to get on with my work.
I want to see what happens next.

His violence wraps me ringside.

In bed, Night 10

That's the problem with you poets. You missed the whole WMD scare (that's weapons of mass destruction — you should listen to the news sometime).

Crow isn't exactly invading Iraq.

Yeah, but you make Crow your mouthpiece.

Crow's involved in what I know.

Tell me you're not putting me into your poems.

We're all implicated.

Let Crow, at least, represent himself.

Writers plunder.

I still don't think it's Crow's job to amplify the six o'clock news.

But he does it so well.

Dream, Night 10

Wing in the dark brushes

my ear. Auditory
flight through the invisible
electromagnetic network
of range finder, mine circuit,
antenna, infrared
night goggles.

Crow picks up
surveillance cameras. Scrambles
navigational systems.
Decodes anti-theft devices.
Nothing looks the way it

sounds. Nothing sounds
how it looks. In the backyard silent
glide

       tucked-in flight feathers — airflow

swooshing the wings.

In the black walnut tree, Night 11

I can almost taste it, says Crow.
The female, the family.
Generations living in peace.

Rid the enemy, that axis
of evil — just one teensy
war and no more bullies
on the playground,
twelve against the native kid
at the swings. No more
motherfucker music till four in the morning,
fist-fights in the hallway.

Hallway?
Is that what
we're fighting for?
A backyard?
Females?
Oil?

Gott Mit Uns proclaimed the belt buckles of the storm troopers.

I need a song, says Crow. A marching drill.
Smoke him out. Bust his ass.
Deck him, drive him, chants Crow,
tapping the slogan
he wears on his favourite sweats: Just do it.

Day 12

What a cleansed
backyard
is worth

is the question Crow doesn't ask.

A world without
difference: Utopia

tempts.

Day 13

Is the strip tease version.

Last night Ted took away the window screen,
propped up a wooden board —
a wedge of mirror remained.

Just past dawn
I'm at the window,

witness
Crow's inky body spilling
over the top of the lumber
for a glimpse
of the bird behind.

Maybe this makes it more exciting —
more like searching than finding.

In Bed, Night 14

> Did you listen to the news?

This a trick question?

No, my answer is no.

> I wanted to see if you were awake.

I am now.

> I did this experiment today. I sprinkled Cheerios on the snow bank.

You're getting attached to this bird.

> He was scared of them.

Come on.

> It's true. He flew away.

Cheerios spooked him?

> He came back once, hovered over the pile, flapped his wings, reduced the forward-flight momentum as if to land —

A kind of weapons inspection.

> Then buggered off.

You're hooked.

> Crow makes the backyard real, like grizzlies in the Rockies —

The mirror can't hold him. He'll tire.

> Some people keep crows as pets.

Try dog food. I hear crows like dog food.

In the black walnut tree, Night 14

How quickly a thing
becomes the thing
you day-to-day do.

And nobody acts as if anything is wrong.
You think it must be you be you be you.

Then something happened.
I saw him, I saw the enemy.
He had a look of shock in his eyes that touched my
shocked inside.

One fleeting but external
point of confirmation
and I saw who I was, what I was doing.
A response I recognized
as clearly as my own reflection
in a pond.

You can trust a pond.

Day 15

A tilted board, a mirror.
Under wisteria vines
a sculpture's snowy base
lies undisturbed.

It was bound to happen.

Small birds go about their business

quietly.

The quiet feels heavy,
much like absence, like missing.

One for sorrow, two.

The day is very quiet.

In the black walnut, Night 15

He can have them. Those
karate-chop moves
weren't that great anyway.
Lots more where they came from.

The thing is, I have good ideas.

And face it, the cheering section —
that woman at the window —
when you're on your game you can feed
off your audience.

Okay, for a while I was caught in the mirror.
I like to think that I advanced the story of Narcissus
preening at pond's edge.
That Greek couldn't attack him-
self, not without
falling in.

And aren't we all
in hot pursuit of our own
buffed reflection?
Don't we bash our heads
against our own inadequacies?

Maybe not you.

But from time to time
I see that woman
fall deeply into her computer screen.

Saved From Drowning

Piet the Bat

1.

My great grandfather drunk-staggered
home so often —
his windmill arms flailing beneath his cape —
they called him Piet the Bat.

Dead at fifty-three.
Two generations later
Peter my father's dying words
to me on a wholly different matter:
Don't tell your mother.

Between their deaths are
my brothers, son, nephews —
knife fights, crushing
machinery, surgeries,
smashed vans and faces.

We don't tell
great grandfather lurching
home to his wife, the potato box
on her black-skirted lap,
the galvanized bucket of water beside her:
plunk potato two potato plunk potato

more. Already seven children.
In this photo the last
child she'll carry is an eye
sprouting in the womb's cellar.

2.

My cape was plaid.
I was pregnant with Cameron,
son who knit himself
inside the wool tent,
into the dark browed family line,
the thick hair, wavy, oh they're handsome,
the Grootendorst men.

Horticulturalists by trade.
The 2001 Southwood rose catalogue lists their line:
rugosa red, Grootendorst pinks.

3.

We children — twig to trunk —
were grafted to what was dearly hoped
and daily prayed to be the safe side
of the ocean, of the story.
Not a whiff of bat.

But Piet darts
out of the black
walnut summer nights
the way a story
will sonar out of the dark
and return to it.

He makes us wild
to thrust our pale sprouts
through burlap. Our way

of begging
for the crack that leads to

light enough to pierce
the story back to Piet
staggering still
canal-side
never falling but
drowning,
and who in the way of drowning men
pulls us, yanks in
our young men.

How I Was Saved From Drowning

This body, the one
waving its arms and drowning,
is mine.

Water storms the vessels
leading into ears
and nose and throat.

So, I'm drowning.
What about my husband, my kids?
My fifteen-year-old son.

My eyes close.

It's fall. We're poking the fire.
My father pulls me into his blanket,
into crooked warmth
and the pipe-smoke smell comes back;
forty years later in this deepest
of silences, it's his smell that

saves me. In the bruising
downward of ocean,
my father's ash-and-fire love
lassoes, ropes me hard,
grows in me
a kind of fin
propeller against the stone

cold, lifts me

up like smoke
like sweet tobacco —

Sixteen Hours After

Sixteen are the hours
it took Dad to catch up to me
when I was born.

Indentured to the farmer,
no telephone, and bicycling
forty-five kilometers
to the Chilliwack General hospital
only after the hay it might rain was in.

Something to do

with the parched smell of July,
the valley, the long
light, heat
bending the hay, but

I remember waiting.

Before We Were People

Crow screams herself hoarse, plunges
her body at thieving
eagle flying hard,
baby bird in its talons —

futile inheritance (thanks
Dad), this love of crows
corvousphilia

kraai in Dutch kraai kraai
this baby meal, this mother-loss
those two black sticks of dangling crow
so newly formed
                about to be dropped
from a dead-head Douglas-fir
further down the beach.

kraai kraai

There are myths about cooking and myths about meat.
Myths about fire and tobacco.
There's a string game played by the Toba Indians.
There's the equatorial sky, the northern sky, the southern cross.
There's my father at the seashore with his pet crow.

Offerings Dad places on the railing —
the bird eating and pooping over the deck,
my mother flapping, Dad crooning, Dad cleaning up.
Who belongs in this story? What are the social
arrangements? Crow shows her back,

then what? Rustic symphony
in three movements: born, eat, die.
From the first we heard music. Divertissement
on a folk theme, bird chorus, a wedding.
Who would have thought that millennia later
a tune would turn up
here on the far side of the world?

Cornelia Hoogland

What you say in any language seems still truer
when the language is music.
1500 centuries later it clings to us —
still in our preferences.

Dad, help me out here: your kraai, my crow.
We were raptors
before we were people. We belonged
to the sky.

Stick to the ground

I advise myself. This story is about meat —
teeth are everywhere.
Snapping shut teeth, tongues,
teeth and gullets and swallowing. Hunger
is rampant. The need
to maim — to pitch
our bodies at chemical lawns,
grenades into buildings.

Dad huffing and puffing
and blowing down
his body, his boat. Red leak in the bow
where the heart is. Hunger

is rampant — the need to devour. To gobble
the earth — where's the music in that?
What are we stalking?

Solo unaccompanied violin — I try to hear crow

speak, try to write
for kids playing tag in perfectly
weed-free lawns. When the world got smoggy
the voice in the head
got loud. I'm listening all the time now.

I'm going to have to write as the salmon fail to spawn,
the bears close in, the fish stocks disappear.
As things heat up.
kraai kraai

I'm going to have to write as the rain falls acid.
Write poems to donate bone marrow by.
Write poems to endure chemotherapy by.
I'm talking writing here, writing poems when you're sick and tired.
Like the forests are sick
and tired.

I know a stand of trees that has seen the gods.
Dad showed me. Crow showed him.

To have been part of that.

Red Painting Shirt

He wears it when he waters the beans,
to lure hummingbirds.
He wants to be touched by the hummers —

Spray high, he says, winging
the garden hose at summer heat.
Three birds dart at the gush.

And when it happens, he says,
that sharp drill you expect and don't expect,
when a hummingbird whizzes your finger —

O, that, his delphinium eyes say,
is the Sistine chapel, God's
ruby throat.

Where We Come From, Where We Go
(Richmond Pavilion, Royal Jubilee Hospital)

1.

Go then with your half-
thoughts, your yellow cab.
8 o'clock is 11 o'clock
three time zones over.
We're alive in different ways.

How it opens
at either end, and the room down the south hall
with facing windows —
where, in bed after giving birth,
I hallucinated roving up and down a ladder,
lusted the midpoint, middle

rung. Brick and mortar
can afford the extremes

of maternity to palliative care.
I was there
when Jack died. He didn't mind
me knitting. Working on the last
sleeve when Death —

a person
about to leap off a tall building.

Somehow, 12 stories below
I knew.

Jack's leave-taking big
as the cow field, ground
of earliest memory.

2.

Osip Mandelstam gave his life for a poem
he couldn't not speak aloud. Informant in the room
but he spoke. His sentence,
the firing squad.

3.

Maya at five years old says that when people die
they go into the ground
and then they go up into the sky where they disappear.
On the word disappear she twirls on one foot
and says, I know this.
I buried a bird and the next day
it was gone. She flutters
her hands, looks up

at them.

4.

You could find yourself

in the cow field. The horizon gave it human
reference. There —

the dividing line, sky

beyond. Air and lemon light.
You knew where you were. You existed.

Or this. Once

in snow, on a white day of no horizon, I floated away.
                              Out among the clouds

I flew on silver string, I flew there and back

to my body.

In Utero

Baby Looks Us Over

Brown chorister
bobs among branches of the Douglas-fir
on the Puntledge.

A paper-
wrapper of a bird,
its small barred wings,
but when it sings, O Mio Babbino —
it's Maria Callas.

Winter wrens cluster
for warmth
like us when baby's born.
We fall in a heap
like birds in a nesting box
mewling and sighing,
exclaiming this full moon
of a girl, this pipit
with the presence
of one who has travelled a great distance,
who arrives
perfectly whole, accepts

the risk.

The Unborn Prepares to Navigate Her Passage Through the Birth Canal

She dreams of kayaking.

Alone at sea level on the west coast,
she looks over the irreducible Pacific
that runs unhindered to the coast of Australia.
All that water. That ways to go.

And the horizon — a stranger
shore. Could it be other-

wise? The wind
kicks up — five-foot waves — but she knows what to do:

align her thighs against the braces, feet against the pegs —
this will torque her round.
Spread-eagle on the rear deck, she'll schlep the boat onto its side.
Allow herself to drop into the water. To be at sea.
And the skills: the hip-snap, the support hand, the assist
hand, the wide swing
to 360 degrees that will roll the kayak.

What do you call that? (She knows there's a word.)
She wants to come out
right, she

        pats her baby palm
        on the water, the sundering sea.

What she must do.

Cornelia Hoogland

And the Rain, and the Sun Coming Out

Finn is the pine needle
the chief's daughter swallowed.
Finn carries the sun
inside her,
carries the theft of the sun
inside her.

Is there a difference?
Finn's already a puzzle.
A good story.

That's her, grinning.

Finn floats in a body
of water, the little wading

pool in the backyard
with an umbrella for sun
where her sister splashes.
Finn hears splashing.

In her studio, that out-building
with the slate path her father laid —
and the goldfinches building a nest in the trellis —
Finn lines up her paints, cleans her brushes, washes the pickle jar.

Finn has an idea —
sticks her hand out the door, checks for

rain
sun breaks

into glitter.

Its scattered reflection.
Its pretty teeth.

Paddling the River

She arrives in her own canoe.
In the sound of a red canoe.

What she must do.

*

The sound of the boat hitting the dock.
In the beginning was donck — the sound
of wood on wood
then silence.

*

Name of the child, name of the parents.
Name of the abnormality
the child is born with,
name of the gene
that took a left turn at 12 weeks gestation,
name of the reasons, the odds, 1 out of 100,000,
name of the savannah — our nameless, barely remembered
relations who walked out of the tall grass —
that's what you think when you see the misshapen hand —
how long we've been at it, this being human.

It's before midnight, the mother's standing
in the hall between the bathroom and the bedroom.
Nothing to do
but watch her baby swim to her husband
who catches his daughter,
who ties off the cord with a shoelace.
And everything goes gooseflesh quiet,

the film grainy — as if the mother's on the far side of glass
she sees past
to the life that's over.

It's not just that glass offers no purchase, but that
she can't read what now separates
her from what she thought she knew
about the world.

It's midnight. She's seeing her baby's hand
for the first time.

Language, I forgive you your puny sticks of meaning,
your weak grasp of the situation.
The crumbs you might have tossed:
she's beautiful, you can rest now, the midwife's on her way.

The midwife.

That's her shooing away the paramedics,
that's her saying time to celebrate.

Woman, attend us
on our journey — remind
mid-aged paddlers on the other side of the country

of the need —

though the river's polluted, the sun over-hot,
though the only sounds are cars, herds of cars,
stampede of just-in-time trucks —

to celebrate.

The name of the river: call it journey, call it life.
Call it the Thames
if that makes you feel better.
Sticks and stones and 40 years
of dumping chemicals
will break my ecosystem —
but names will never
hurt me, says the river, fingers crossed.

We start paddling, we enter the river.
Easy for us — it's downstream from here.
The current leads and we steer
among dead heads, fallen logs, small rapids.

The baby girl enters the same day we do, we're in it together.
Born with the j-stroke, the draw, the pry
in bone and muscle.

The newborn enters the river.

Littoral

lit·to·ral (adj)
on or near a shore, especially the zone between the high and
low tide marks

Crow's On My Mind: Three Poems

1. The Sky is Falling

Cacophonous, crows
heading to the roost against
the sky, early evening.

Used to be. Last seen
flying over urban sprawl along the 401.

Ah but we're here. Our black shirts for anarchy.

And yes — this morning at first light
twenty, maybe. Intelligent as arrows —
black and straight. Crow's signature
against the sky, the Pink Pearl

eraser sky.

2. Crow is Medieval

The way those folk suffered the body —
once described by Kenneth Clarke as a bulb
dug up by mistake, a sad thing,
a tuber clotted with sin.

Larval, we human
worms who can't wait
to pupate

into butterflies for God
way up there in the gothic arches, way up, way way up.

3. The Sound of Crow Belongs

to the cold
the raw
the hinge-day

winter ratcheting
its rusty
lever into the next season.

You smell
the earth faintly
breathing beneath the snow
receding

hear crow's

aw
aw
aw

anguish
or openmouthed prayer.

Hard-Wired

The boy is walking on snow,
on a ridge of snow

beside a plowed sidewalk
on which he should be walking
yells the daycare worker from the head

of the rope the children clutch
at intervals, a zigzag snake, intermittent flashes
of red, blue and yellow, a kind of theatre —

except it's a safety device, nothing magical about it — ya listening?

No, he's not. The Puntledge River
is on the boy's mind.
                        He picks up
the deer trail beside it, walks
on fir needle, bear scat and rotting fish
that create the earth

beneath his boots. Dirt
holds him, supplies reason
he's here. Each footstep
roots his understanding, shapes

his metaphor. Day after day
he's watched the spawning salmon disintegrate,
leak their nutrients into the soil
that furnish the cedars, the White Pine. He can tell you
how it works: that wolves eat only the heads of fish
they carry back to their dens. Whole forests get fertilized this way.

But he's back at daycare with his evolutionary desire
to test himself against the elements:
snow seems too slight to hold his weight but does.
Crunching sounds
he'll remember in grade 8 during the poetry assignment.

Just now it's mathematical tricks,
the way his foot prints an angle, a whole series of angles.

Cornelia Hoogland

What She Makes Of It

Because you broke my heart, she says,

below battered
gold October mountains.

You have to look hard
to see what the three-year-old makes
of the shiny thing lost
from somebody's dollar store crown
among beach stones.

Between pinched thumb and finger
it's become story. Tiny,
very tiny, the glitter
of her abandonment,
the green jewel —

is for you, she says.

Guide to the River

1.

Oneida children greet the eight Nova Craft canoes —
red and blue and green — arriving on shore.
Seventeen mid-aged paddlers, stinking and sunburned.
Such arrival has happened before. Gifts
of guns and disease.

But these are savvy kids, they snap us up
from behind the viewfinders of their digital cameras;
our fold-up chairs in their lenses.
Their fathers drive us through the planted field —
rows of ripening corn under the truck tires,
corn that will spring back up, they tell us —

they should know —

to the cookhouse where Annie and the women
prepare venison and bannock.
Pointing and laughing the children download
shots of us they've captured —

we barely recognize. It's hard
to go back, to turn around
in a boat — easier to sit facing forward
and let the world come to you for naming.

2.

Askunessippi, 'the antlered river,' named by the Attawandaron,
the original inhabitants.

Renamed La Tranche, 'ditch' in French.

Renamed Thames River, 'the River Thames in England'
by Lieutenant Governor John Graves Simcoe in 1793.

3.

River's putty fingers, trailings
of strawberries.
                    Clay bank
and clay water, cold slip
labours the bank to the cow field, the corn.

Turtles — snapping and painted —
scud across its surfaces.

In the morning the elegant five fingered
print of raccoon,
at the waters' clay edge the split heart
shape of the buck's
cloven hoof. Cougar paw prints
at the overturned canoe.

Wet mud, glissando, glissade — we lose our grip.

Fundamental

It was a tsunami. We were hoping for nothing
but sun
and to get through Naomi Klein's newest fat book. The wasps
found the thawing chicken. A blue tension
hovered, lifted
its four separate wings
and batted over the pond. The dragonflies
fell into Snowbirds formation.

My sister roared into camp,
threw open the car door,
said the water in Whaling Station Bay
was receding at an alarming
rate all the way to Texada.
The bay sucked dry,
whales and sea lions uncovered,
everything revealed. Eels from their caves.
Then the onrush — wall of water surging
inland. It was fascinating.

Get the fuck in, we're heading to Mt. Geoffrey, she said,
the only safe place on the island.

What I remember of summer is how tired
my sister was of saving the world.

                 The radio's saying
Israel resealed its border with Gaza this morning.
That's what the radio calls it — resealed border —
but I see security barriers rigged
parallel to the 401 — concrete walls
higher than your head,
the just-in-time trucks and eighteen-wheelers pressing
                 close, pressing in.

She Questions Her Work

Dusk falls over the house.
In the yard the puffy, rushing
sound of a hot-air balloon.
Her husband's letting air
out of his compressor.
Somebody on the radio says that's all for today.

Three police cars and an ambulance
drive into the parking lot of the tenement
house across the street.

Light recedes by pin pricks.

Sometimes it's Alex, her neighbour, staggering home
in his pyjama bottoms.

A group gathers. People touch each other.

Bob the gravedigger says
people give up
when the seasonal hinge cracks
open. Spring
close but no cigar.

Cold sharpens everything.

A tall thin man she's never seen before
walks out of the apartment between officers
into the ambulance. It drives off
and the police go back into the building
and the clumps of people, river water
thickened with cold, break up, drift away.

The supper-hour traffic a block over on Wharncliffe
is what you'd expect.

In the Current One Discovers the Immense Passage

Travis puts down his seminar paper. He's talking
about birds in literature — paper swallow, paper swift —
when he stops speaking and makes the sound

that the white-throated sparrow makes.

Concentrates us on the bird's hollow-reed song and air
surges into the room: air for the bird, air for its sound.
Oxygen into the lungs of the people listening —
and the roof lifts off room 222 University College.

Travis starts reading to us again but
impossible to stay put. The sky pouring in.

Cornelia Hoogland

A Man at His Keyboard Orbits the World

The CD over, quiet
rushes the room.

The lake in winter.

Dante said that after the dream,
passion endures, imprinted.
Droplets of sweetness, he said.

Below the ice, susurrating waves.

High above, the sun's
production of hydrogen into helium;
400 million tons per second,
four of which convert to photons
that stream through space

to light earth's surfaces — snow's
falling and lifting, its sideways
maneuvers.

The solar give-away
illuminates our galaxy

where there's a time capsule
NASA set spinning.
Included in that hope
chest is a silver wafer
of Glenn Gould (his containment, the distance
he had from people)
playing the Goldberg Variations.

A CD floats in space. The deep space

between each
of his notes.

Crow

There is nothing for tart absence
but to acknowledge
the changes.

Take this bramble rap-
acious over the path,

blackberries ripening —
green to red to bursting — all week
when her house glowed
with company and she didn't need

to notice.

Now she's heading to the water.
Now she's carrying on
with just the dog.
Sound of a distant train.

In the high branch of Douglas-fir
hangs the daytime moon, mostly
unseen, always
there. In the barbed thorn, crow.

       Caw caw caw.

Fat, sugar-baited berry.
Flash of oil in the ditch.

       Okay okay I see you

spring from waste
and prickle,

glint of sun on your beak.

Acknowledgements

Ted Hughes, of course. His *Crow: From the Life and Songs of a Crow* (London: Faber, 1970). I am also indebted to Bernd Heinrich's *Mind of the raven: investigations and adventures with wolf-birds* (New York: Cliff Street Books, 1999), and Canada's beloved bird man, Don McKay.

Thank you to the Ontario Arts Council, the Canada Council, the League of Canadian Poets, the Banff Centre for the Arts, and the University of Western Ontario for support (financial and otherwise), and to my writing community — Marty Gervais and the people at Black Moss Press, especially my wonderful editor, Jasmine Elliott, and Kate Hargreaves, designer. Gerry Shikatani, for your earlier reading of "Tar Baby." Karen Schindler, as always, thank you.

The cover crow is a detail from Colleen Couves's *Crow Vision 1*. Her visual art can be viewed at colleencouves.com. Thank you, Colleen.

I am grateful to the small presses and anthologies that have published many of the poems in this book, including: the *Malahat Review*'s Green Imagination (J. Ruzesky, ed.); *Regreen; New Canadian Ecological Poetry* (M. Anand and A. Dickinson, eds.); *White ink: poems on mothers and motherhood* (R. Dunlop, ed.); League of Canadian poets' *And nobody knows the blood we share* (Anne Burke, ed.); *The River Project: 19 London Artists Turn to the Thames* (Herman Goodden, ed.); *Dream Catcher: Canadian Issue*, 23; *The Fiddlehead; The Saving Bannister Literary Anthology*, Vol.23; *Hammered Out* #12; *The 2007 Silver Hammer Awards Anthology; The Antigonish Review; Literary Review of Canada; Descant; Windsor Review; Mothering, Sex and Sexuality; Anderbo Poetry* (US); *Poetry in Motion* and *The New Quarterly*.

Cornelia Hoogland

Poems that have won awards or have been shortlisted for awards include:

"Baby looks us over" finalist, *Anderbo* poetry competition, U.S., 2011

"Poet's Familiar" finalist, *Descant's* Winston Collins Best Canadian Poem, 2008

"Piet the Bat" 1st place, St. Catharines Authors Association Anthology, 2008

"Wo ist Die Wolle" 1st place, Silver Hammer Anthology, *Hammered Out*, Hamilton, ON., 2007

"Tar Baby" finalist, CBC Literary Awards, 2006

"My Mother meets Ted" in "Second Marriage" 1st place, Canadian Poetry Association's Basmajian Award Chapbook, 2005.

In the poem titled "The Sky Is Falling" I am indebted to Fanny Howe's poem, "O'Clock." The title "In the Current One Discovers the Immense Passage," is a quote from Luce Irigaray.

Ted Goodden, my constant reader.
I give you "thanks;" you give me "thrive."